LIVING WITH
EATING DISORDERS

ABDO
Publishing Company

LIVING WITH EATING DISORDERS

by Racquel Foran

Content Consultant
Kathleen Kara Fitzpatrick, PhD, Clinical Assistant Professor,
Stanford Medical Center/Lucile Packard Children's Hospital

LIVING WITH HEALTH CHALLENGES

CREDITS

Published by ABDO Publishing Company, PO Box 398166, Minneapolis, MN 55439. Copyright © 2014 by Abdo Consulting Group, Inc. International copyrights reserved in all countries. No part of this book may be reproduced in any form without written permission from the publisher. The Essential Library™ is a trademark and logo of ABDO Publishing Company.

Printed in the United States of America,
North Mankato, Minnesota
092013
012014

 THIS BOOK CONTAINS AT LEAST 10% RECYCLED MATERIALS.

Editor: Jenna Gleisner
Series Designer: Becky Daum

Photo credits: Shutterstock Images, cover, 3, 48, 58, 75, 80, 95; Thinkstock, 8, 15, 32, 56, 72, 78; iStockphoto, 10, 23, 46, 52, 68, 70, 88; Aleksander Markin/Shutterstock Images, 12; Jason Stitt/Shutterstock Images, 20; Evan Agostini/AP Images, 27; Andrey Shadrin/Shutterstock Images, 37; Mariusz S. Jurgielewicz/Shutterstock Images, 39; Diego Cervo/iStockphoto, 42; Jaimie Duplass/Shutterstock Images, 50; Warren Goldswain/Shutterstock Images, 64; Petrenko Andriy/Shutterstock Images, 84; Solovyova Lyudmyla/Shutterstock Images, 92

Library of Congress Control Number: 2013945898

Cataloging-in-Publication Data

Foran, Racquel.
 Living with eating disorders / Racquel Foran.
   p. cm. -- (Living with health challenges)
Includes bibliographical references and index.
ISBN 978-1-62403-245-5
1. Eating disorders--Juvenile literature.   I. Title.
616.85--dc23

                                                          2013945898

CONTENTS

EXPERT ADVICE

I am an attending and clinic manager for the Stanford University/Lucile Packard Children's Hospital Eating Disorders Clinic. I have been working exclusively with a child and adolescent eating disordered population since 2005. During that time, I have served as a research therapist and developer in several large-scale clinical trials, comparing family-based therapy (FBT or "Maudsley") to individual treatment in adolescent anorexia nervosa. I am a supervisor and trainer in FBT and am certified in adolescent focused psychotherapy (AFT), cognitive behavioral therapy (CBT), and interpersonal therapy (IPT) for adolescents with bulimia.

Through my experience, I have noted that anorexia nervosa, in particular, is a disorder of adolescence. Adolescence is also a time of rapid physical and cognitive change, which places many adolescents at risk for eating disorders. My advice to teens is to renourish. The brain is compromised in eating disorders, and good, continuous renourishment is essential to recovery. Staying in a healthy weight range is critical to recovery. The foods that are often the most challenging are also the most important to restoring health in a malnourished body: fats and proteins. Growing bodies must have available energy to promote growth, pubertal changes, and continued cognitive development.

Also, know that it gets better. If you get help—and you can—there are treatments that can get a full cure. Even though you may read stories on the Internet or in other places that say people never recover from eating disorders, that isn't true. In fact, adolescents have an even better response to treatment than adults! You are not alone.

I love working with teenagers with eating disorders because, as a group, teens are some of the smartest, most passionate, interesting, and awesome people. It can be hard to be all of that in the grips of an eating disorder, but when you push past it, when you stop letting it bully you, when you stop buying in to the concept that "being less of a body is being more of a person," you can find that life is an amazing, delightful journey. It is my privilege to be along for the ride.

— *Kathleen Kara Fitzpatrick, PhD*
Clinical Assistant Professor of Psychiatry and
Behavioral Science
Stanford Medical Center/Lucile Packard Children's
Hospital

WARNING SIGNS AND SYMPTOMS

Three months ago, Gabriella had looked at herself in the studio's full-length mirror. To her, it looked like her leotard was pinching her thighs. Every other girl in her ballet class was so tall and skinny. Their legs looked so thin. Why hadn't she grown into a beanpole

Certain sports and activities that highlight physical appearance, such as ballet, can place added stress on teens to look a certain way.

this year like all of the other girls? Now that she was in high school, the pressure to improve and win competitions was mounting. She had to look good on the floor, and she decided looking good meant looking skinny. She was only 100 pounds (45 kg), but she decided to go on a diet.

Gabriella had been on her diet for three months. The first month she cut out junk food, but that didn't drop her weight fast enough. So she started cutting her portions. By the third month, Gabriella was only eating one-eighth of a cup of yogurt with one strawberry for breakfast, a cup of green salad with no dressing for lunch, and maybe another small salad for dinner. If she felt hungry, she drank water.

Now it was time for the first competition of the year. Gabriella hadn't eaten for the past day and a half. She had to look perfect for this performance. Gabriella had felt so tired lately, but it was her time to show everyone how skinny she was and how great she looked as a thin dancer. She stepped out onto the stage. The lights dimmed, but they still seemed so bright. Her music started, but she could hardly hear it. She started seeing spots. "I can't faint today!" she thought. She told herself she could eat after the routine.

Many eating disorder sufferers see a distorted image of themselves and are dissatisfied with the way they look.

DEFINING EATING DISORDERS

Gabriella fainted before she could even start her routine. She was diagnosed with anorexia nervosa, an eating disorder that afflicts one in every 200 women in the United States.[1] As many as 24 million people of all ages and genders suffer from an eating disorder—anorexia, bulimia, binge eating disorder, or other—in the United States alone.[2]

To have an eating disorder is to have an unhealthy relationship with food. This can include eating too much, not eating enough, eating selectively, or binge eating. People who have an eating disorder are also likely to be depressed, have low self-esteem, and tend to be dissatisfied with their body shape or size. Eating disorders are considered mental illnesses, and they are among the most dangerous of all mental illnesses.

The *Diagnostic and Statistical Manual of Mental Disorders, Fifth Edition* (*DSM-5*) defines a number of disorders under the category of eating: anorexia nervosa, bulimia, avoidant/restrictive food intake disorder, and binge eating, which is not to be confused with overeating—something most people do occasionally. All other eating-related disorders that do not match the diagnostic criteria of one of these disorders are categorized as feeding and eating conditions not elsewhere classified (FEC NEC).

EATING DISORDER CHANGES IN THE *DSM-5*

The *DSM-5* now includes binge eating disorder as its own category, but in previous editions it fell in the category of eating disorders not otherwise specified (EDNOS). The change was made to help differentiate patients who simply overeat from those who suffer from recurrent binge eating. The new edition of the manual also changed EDNOS to FEC NEC. Amenorrhea was removed as a criterion for diagnosing anorexia. One reason for this change was that amenorrhea excluded males from being diagnosed anorexic. Avoidant/restrictive food intake disorder was also added as its own category.

Anorexia athletica is most commonly found in elite athletes, who strive for perfection.

The FEC NEC umbrella includes informal subcategories including anorexia athletica, which is also sometimes called compulsive exercising or sports anorexia. Athletica is characterized by excessive, obsessive exercise and insufficient nourishment. Another FEC NEC is night eating, characterized by consuming the majority of one's daily calories in the evening or at night, which leads to sleep disruptions and obesity. Orthorexia relates to restricting eating to self-defined "right" or "proper" foods. All eating disorders should be taken seriously. Even if you see behaviors that may look insignificant, they can lead to very serious health issues for some people.

SYMPTOMS

Differentiating a serious eating disorder from a temporary phase can sometimes be difficult. Many children are fussy eaters. People sometimes choose vegetarianism and veganism for ethical or health reasons. Sometimes shifting diet habits is a good change. Knowing the difference between normal and problematic is important. The most serious and prevalent eating disorders do present some clear signs you can watch for.

NIGHT EATING SYNDROME

One eating disorder that falls in the FEC NEC category is night eating syndrome (NES). Although it does not fall into its own category, medical professionals are increasingly seeing the link between NES, obesity, and binge eating. Research has shown night eaters usually eat the majority of their daily calories between 8:00 p.m. and 6:00 a.m., when their bodies don't burn calories as quickly. Their nighttime snacks also tend to be high in carbohydrates and low in protein, which throws off sugar and hormone levels. The primary physical complication related to NES is obesity. Up to 40 percent of night eaters seeking treatment for obesity also engage in episodes of binge eating.[3]

AVOIDANT/RESTRICTIVE FOOD INTAKE DISORDER

Avoidant/restrictive food intake disorder is listed in the *DSM-4* as an eating disorder of infancy or childhood. In the *DSM-5*, the disorder is expanded to include a wider range of disordered behavior that is not necessarily exclusive to children. Examples of avoidant or restrictive behavior include eating only food of certain colors or textures. Picky eating is common in children, but if extreme, it can lead to both nutritional and psychological problems.

ANOREXIA NERVOSA

A person with anorexia will develop an obsession with his or her weight, believing he or she is fat and needs to lose weight regardless of whether this is true. If you have anorexia, some of your behaviors may include restricting calories, obsessively measuring portions, eating only specific foods, and skipping entire meals on a daily basis for an extended period of time. A medical professional diagnoses anorexia if the patient has a distorted body image, a fear of becoming fat, and diets excessively to the point of severe weight loss. Body mass index (BMI) is the most common measurement used to determine someone's appropriate weight. BMI is calculated by dividing weight in pounds by height in inches squared and multiplying by a conversion factor of 703.

Those with anorexia nervosa are very particular about when and what they consume, often cutting down meals to very unhealthy portions.

If caught early, anorexia can be treated, but if not treated, ongoing malnutrition can do extreme damage to the body. The long-term health consequences of anorexia include the growth of fine hair over the face, arms, and back. This condition, called lanugo, is the body's instinctive way of keeping warm and protecting itself from the cold as it loses fat and muscle. Vitamin deficiencies cause head hair loss, dry skin, and brittle nails. Other symptoms include thinning bones, loss of muscle, low blood pressure, lethargy, heart damage, multiorgan failure, and, in too many cases, death.

BULIMIA

Bulimia is often not quite as easy to identify as anorexia because those who suffer from it aren't necessarily underweight; sometimes they are even overweight. People who suffer from bulimia engage in a repeated pattern of eating large amounts of food followed by immediate purging, which is most often forced vomiting. Other methods of purging include excessive use of diet pills, laxatives, and diuretics. Much like anorexics, bulimics often have an obsession with gaining weight, want to lose weight, and are extremely unhappy with their body shape and size.

If you are bulimic, you may also suffer from long-term symptoms including chronically inflamed and sore throat and acid reflux disorder. Acid reflux occurs when stomach acid travels up your esophagus. Both this and the sore throat are caused by frequent vomiting. Constant vomiting can also destroy tooth enamel, causing your teeth to decay and crumble. Gastrointestinal problems, swollen salivary glands, and severe dehydration caused from continual purging of body fluids are also common. Purging can cause body minerals to become imbalanced. Minerals such as potassium, sodium, calcium, and magnesium, help trigger and conduct electric impulses in the heart.

The unpleasant behaviors of bulimia often cause feelings of shame and embarrassment, so they are often kept secret. One of the most obvious signs someone may be suffering from bulimia is if he or she eats very large meals

> ## WORD ORIGINS
>
> **The words *anorexia* and *bulimia* are of Greek origin. Anorexia comes from the words *an*, or "without," and *orexis*, or "appetite," and bulimia comes from the words *bou*, or "ox," and *limos*, or "hunger," or less literally "ravenous hunger."**

and then immediately goes to the bathroom when finished. Bulimics are usually able to hide their problem for a long time because of their embarrassment.

BINGE EATING DISORDER

Among eating disorders, binge eating disorder (BED) is the most common, although not among youth. The *DSM-5* defines binge eating as "recurring episodes of eating significantly more food in a short period of time than most people would eat under similar circumstances, with episodes marked by feelings of lack of control."[4] The behavior must occur at least once a week for a period of three months for a person to be clinically diagnosed as a binge eater.

If you binge eat, you might not show outward physical signs or symptoms, but there are several behaviors that indicate a problem. Eating unusually large amounts of food, eating even when not hungry, feeling no control over eating, eating until uncomfortably full, and eating alone and feeling depressed or ashamed while doing so are all strong indicators of a binge eating disorder.

Unlike bulimics, binge eaters do not purge after their episodes of overeating, so they are often overweight or obese. This can have a devastating impact on the body, although as with binge eaters, the effects can take years to present themselves. Binge eating can lead to cardiovascular disease, high blood pressure, high cholesterol, and type 2 diabetes. Much like bulimics, binge eaters may feel guilt,

STATISTICS SHOW UNHEALTHY TREND

Statistics show Americans have an increasingly unhealthy relationship with food. Sixty-one percent of American adults are overweight, and one in five is classified as obese, with a BMI of 30 or greater.[5] And it's not just adults. Each generation is heavier than the previous one. According to the Centers for Disease Control and Prevention (CDC), childhood obesity has tripled since 1980. Roughly 31 percent of US children and teens were overweight or obese in 2008.[6] At the same time, it is estimated 10 to 15 percent of all Americans suffer from some type of serious eating disorder.[7]

embarrassment, and disgust and keep their behaviors a secret.

ASK YOURSELF THIS

- *In what ways can you imagine Gabriella's life changing if she continues starving herself?*

- *Do you have a friend you think might be anorexic or bulimic? What behaviors make you think so?*

- *Why do you think it is so difficult for people with eating disorders to admit they have a problem?*

- *Have you been in a situation in which you felt fat or self-conscious about your looks? What did you do and why?*

- *Have you ever considered taking extreme measures to lose weight? What made you think you needed to do this?*

CAUSES AND RISK FACTORS

L evi had always been hard on himself. He had plenty of wrestling trophies to prove it. But lately, he felt as though he needed to prove himself to his coach and teammates. Last month his coach made jokes in front of the whole team, saying, "Levi seems to have

gotten soft over the summer." After practice, his
coach even asked Levi if he would be able to cut
the weight he needed to wrestle in his weight
division. That was when Levi started showing up
at the gym an hour before practice to do extra
weight training. His coach and his teammates
started commenting on his more muscular
physique, so he started sticking around after
practice to lift even more weights and run a few
extra miles around the track.

A month into his new routine, Levi had
everyone from teammates to girls at school
noticing his build. He must be doing something
right, he thought. His confidence was building,
and he was winning more matches than the
previous year.

But tonight at weigh-in, he was five pounds
(2.3 kg) heavier. He had been working out like
crazy. How could he be gaining weight? As he
scooped another heap of mashed potatoes onto
his plate, Levi's mom picked up on his mood.
"Don't eat your feelings now, Levi," she joked.
"It's just a number. I'm sure you'll make the
weight in no time, with the way you're working
out." But Levi didn't take her comment as a joke.
After dinner he locked himself in his bathroom.
He turned the shower on, but instead of getting
in, he hovered over the toilet. Putting his fingers

down his throat, Levi forced himself to throw up the mashed potatoes and steak he'd just eaten.

A MULTITUDE OF RISK FACTORS

Levi didn't know it, but his chosen sport— combined with his personality—put him at high risk for developing an eating disorder, in his case, bulimia. As with many mental illnesses, what causes someone to develop an eating disorder is often difficult to determine. There are, however, risk factors and certain commonalities among people who suffer from eating disorders.

Age, gender, and both biological and environmental factors can all play a role in whether you acquire an eating disorder. Research shows those who have a parent, sibling, or child with an eating disorder are more

ATHLETES AT RISK

Certain sports have a higher eating disorder risk factor associated with them. Research has shown there is a 13 percent prevalence of eating disorders associated with sports in which participants are judged and scored, versus only 3 percent in refereed sports. Elite female athletes show an even higher tendency toward eating disorders at 20 percent, compared with 9 percent in the control group.[1] And female athletes who participate in visually artistic sports such as gymnastics, ballet, and figure skating are at the highest risk of all. One explanation for this could be found in the personality similarities many athletes and anorexics share: perfectionism, high self-expectations, competitiveness, hyperactivity, and compulsiveness.

Studies have shown if one identical twin has an eating disorder, the twin sibling is likely to have one as well.

prone to both anorexia and bulimia. Those who participate in certain sports and activities and individuals with specific psychiatric personality disorders can also be at higher risk for eating disorders. What all experts agree on is that the absolute cause is not known and much more research is needed.

FEMALE ATHLETE TRIAD

It is common for young female athletes to work to maintain a low body weight so they can postpone puberty and keep a boyish figure. The term *female athlete triad* is used to describe athletes who engage in this behavior. It is a combination of three conditions: disordered eating, amenorrhea, and osteoporosis.

ETHNICITY, GENDER, AND AGE

Studies have suggested eating disorders are most common in women from developed Western nations, including the United States, Canada, Europe, Australia, New Zealand, and South Africa. In the United States, eating disorders afflict Latin-American, African-American, and Native-American women, but they occur in white women more often. Eating disorders do however seem to be spreading beyond Western countries. A 2007 study from the Chinese University of Hong Kong showed that the number of eating disorder patients in Hong Kong doubled in a ten-year period.[2]

It is also a fact that more females than males report eating disorders. Only 10 to 15 percent of people with anorexia or bulimia and 40 percent of diagnosed binge eaters are males.[3] However, no one is sure how accurate these statistics are, as males tend to report less often because they consider eating disorders a female problem. One survey of 131 Cornell University football players revealed 40 percent of the respondents engaged in bingeing and purging behaviors, and 10 percent of those were classified as having a clinical eating disorder.[4]

Dr. Blake Woodside, the director of the eating disorders program at Toronto General Hospital in Toronto, Canada, agrees eating disorders are much more common in males than many expect. According to Dr. Woodside, community-based studies indicate one out of every three cases of anorexia and one out of four cases of bulimia are male.[5] Many males disguise their bulimia as staying in shape, and they exercise compulsively as a way of purging. So although it may appear more females suffer from eating disorders, there is no doubt males are also at risk.

Eating disorders occur most often in adolescents, with 86 percent of people with eating disorders reporting the onset by the time they were 20 years old.[6] Much like gender, however, it is not an exclusive club. Children are starting to diet at much younger ages, and eating disorders are becoming more common in younger children. Older adults can also have an eating disorder that has lingered. Binge eating disorder, which is more common than anorexia and bulimia, is more prevalent in adults. One in 35 adults in the United States has binge eating disorder. Binge eating is also different in that it doesn't discriminate against gender or race; 40 percent of cases are men, and just as many African American and Hispanic women have binge eating disorder as do white women.[7]

SOCIAL FACTORS

When the clinical diagnosis of anorexia was first formalized in 1874, it was considered a "nervous" disease. When Sir William Withey Gull first reported his research to the Clinical Society of London, he called the disorder anorexia nervosa, which literally translates to "nervous loss of appetite." It was common for it to be characterized as a behavior young women chose to engage in for emotional and attention-seeking reasons. With an increase in cases, anorexia nervosa was finally recognized as a psychiatric disorder in 1980. However, because eating disorders increased in the late 1900s, they afflicted more women than men, and they were more prevalent in Western countries, researchers have focused on social factors as a major cause.

Many believe eating disorders have become more common in young Western women because of the media. Images in magazines, on

Ignoring body image can be difficult when popular culture glorifies thin celebrities and role models.

television, in movies, and now on the Internet all tend to associate beauty with being thin. Although there is no research to support a direct causal link between media images and messaging and eating disorders, it is still felt they can have a compounding impact on some

DIETING AND EATING DISORDERS

Dieting, or changing one's eating and exercise habits to lose weight, has become an epidemic in the United States. At any given time, there are approximately 46 million men and 69 million women dieting to either lose weight or maintain their current weight. This represents approximately 55 percent of the adult population.[8] Why does all of this dieting pose a problem? Of those so-called normal dieters, 35 percent become pathological dieters, and 20 to 25 percent of those acquire an eating disorder.[9]

people. When media constantly idealize a certain body type as perfect, teens who don't have that body type are inclined to feel less than perfect. Those who develop eating disorders tend to overvalue the perfect image and make extreme attempts to achieve that ideal.

PSYCHOLOGICAL FACTORS

If social factors are causing eating disorders, then why doesn't more of the population suffer from them? Studies have shown psychological factors also play a role. People with eating disorders often have other personality traits and disorders in common, including depression; avoidant personality disorder, in which individuals are extremely socially inhibited and very sensitive to criticism to the point of social isolation; narcissistic personality, which is characterized by an inflated sense of self-importance and an extreme need for admiration; and other anxiety disorders such as panic disorder and phobias.

There is a strong correlation between obsessive compulsive disorder (OCD) and both anorexia and bulimia. OCD occurs in up to two-thirds of patients with anorexia or bulimia.[10] People who have both anorexia and OCD tend to become compulsive about dieting and exercise. They develop extreme rituals such as cutting their food into tiny pieces or chewing every bite a certain number of times. Some believe eating disorders are just another way OCD manifests itself.

GENETIC AND BIOLOGICAL FACTORS

Researchers have also started examining genetic and biological factors. One study found relatives of anorexics and bulimics had an increased risk of an eating disorder. This led researchers to conclude there is a familial link for anorexia nervosa and bulimia. The problem researchers have is determining what is caused by environment and what is caused by genetics. Researchers study both identical and fraternal twins to help make this differentiation.

Twin studies look at similarities, or concordance, between twin pairs, such as height or disorders. If concordance is similar between both identical and fraternal twins, then the similarity is attributed to them having been raised in the same environment. If, however, identical twins show greater concordance with a disorder than fraternal twins, the similarity is attributed to genes. Studies have shown identical twins have greater concordance for eating disorders, meaning that if one identical twin has an eating disorder, the other twin is likely to test similarly. This has provided researchers with evidence that genes do play a role in whether an individual will develop an eating disorder. What this all means is that there is no one single factor that brings on an eating disorder but rather a combination of factors.

SPRING BIRTH CONNECTION

In 2011, Dr. Lahiru Handunnetthi of the Wellcome Trust Centre for Human Genetics at Oxford University led a research team that compared the birth dates of 1,293 patients with anorexia to those of the general population. They found there were more anorexics born between March and June and a deficit of anorexics born from September to October.[11] The study shows evidence of an association, but it doesn't explain what is putting people born in the spring at higher risk. Previous studies have shown other mental disorders are also more commonly found in those born in the spring.

ASK YOURSELF THIS

- *How do you think Levi's coach's comment affected Levi's development of an eating disorder?*

- *Do you think it is appropriate for coaches in sports such as wrestling to pressure athletes to achieve a certain weight?*

- *What impact do you think Levi's choice of sport had on him developing an eating disorder?*

- *Do you think that if someone has a family member with an eating disorder, all other members of the family are at risk? Do you think social factors affect one's chances of developing an eating disorder? Why or why not?*

- *Do you think there is more or less pressure on boys than girls to have the "right" body type, and why?*

- *Have you ever had someone tell you you should lose weight? If so, how did this make you feel, and how did you respond?*

COMPLICATIONS

Jennifer's mother had been calling her for ten minutes now, and Jennifer knew if she didn't get downstairs her mother would come up. But she couldn't figure out what to wear. Almost every item of clothing she owned was piled on the bed behind her. Everything

Some anorexics wear loose-fitting clothing to cover up and hide the changes to their bodies.

made her feel ugly. All of her pants were too big for her. She had been dieting for several months. She loved her new skinny body, but it was tough to find clothes that fit. To make things even more difficult, she felt like she had to wear long sleeves. In the last month, her arms had become hairy, or as her best friend Meg had described them, "fluffy."

Her mother called again, so Jennifer pulled on a pair of black leggings and a baggy sweatshirt and ran downstairs. The minute her mother saw her, she asked, "Why are you dressed like that? You will die of heat." Jennifer told her mother all her clothes were dirty and walked out of the house. Her mother's last words followed her down the path: "You didn't eat breakfast again."

"That was the plan," Jennifer thought to herself. She also didn't bring a lunch; she had no plans to eat today. She still wanted to lose five more pounds.

As always, Meg met her at the halfway point on the walk to school. "Hey Jen, why you dressed like an Eskimo today? Trying to cover up those fluffy arms of yours?" Meg asked while laughing. But Jennifer didn't think it was funny. It was worse than Meg knew. Jennifer had fluffy hair all over her back now, and she was starting to get it on her face, too. She had no idea why it was happening, and she hoped nobody else would notice.

TRADING LIFE YEARS FOR THE IDEAL BODY

A group of British undergraduates conducted a survey at the University of West England. The group asked women if they would be willing to trade years of their lives in exchange for their ideal body shape and weight. Sixteen percent of the respondents said they would trade one year; 10 percent were willing to trade two to five years; 2 percent were willing to trade up to ten years; and 1 percent said they would give up 21 years or more.[1]

A VERY SERIOUS DIAGNOSIS

What Jennifer didn't know yet was that her dieting had developed into anorexia, and she was experiencing one of many potential complications from the disorder: lanugo. Being diagnosed with an eating disorder is very serious. At best, anorexia, bulimia, and binge eating can cause manageable medical conditions. At worst, these disorders can cause death. The three clinically defined eating disorders can all lead to kidney problems, heart conditions, and a number of psychological disorders, including depression and anxiety, but each also presents its own set of complications.

COMPLICATIONS FROM ANOREXIA

Once you start starving your body of essential nutrients, this malnutrition can cause your body to respond and behave in strange ways. Lanugo can begin to grow on your face, arms, and back. Dehydration from restricting fluid intake brings out dark circles under your eyes, causing your face to look sunken. Cramping and bloating of the stomach as well as diarrhea are also common. Constipation is another problem; this is usually caused by overuse of laxatives, which damages the nerves of the colon and leads to permanent constipation.

Malnourishment can also harm every organ in the body. In addition to kidney damage, it can lead to respiratory infections, pancreas failure,

THE FIRST FACE OF ANOREXIA

As is often the case with unfamiliar or unpleasant topics, anorexia was not in the public conscience for a long time. If someone knew someone with a problem, it was kept quiet and addressed privately. It wasn't until pop music superstar Karen Carpenter died of anorexia in 1983 that people really started paying attention to the disorder. Before her death, no one talked about it. Since Carpenter's death, many celebrities, including pop singers Lady Gaga, Kelly Clarkson, and Lily Allen, actress Mary-Kate Olsen, and even the late Princess Diana of England have come forward and admitted to having had an eating disorder.

ELECTROLYTES

Electrolytes are essential minerals in the blood stream and body fluids that conduct electricity. The minerals include potassium, sodium, chloride, calcium, magnesium, bicarbonate, phosphate, and sulfate. Balanced electrolytes are key to your health. For example, an abnormal increase or decrease in potassium levels can impact the nervous system, increasing the chance of irregular heartbeats, which can be fatal. The movement of sodium also plays an important role in generating the electrical signals required for the brain, nervous system, and muscles to communicate.

infertility, and even blindness. Anorexia can also lead to electrolyte imbalance. Electrolyte levels that are out of balance can cause irregular heartbeats, chest pain, heart attack, and heart failure, leading to death. Even when anorexia is treated and under control, the damage done is often irreversible.

COMPLICATIONS FROM BULIMIA

The pattern of bingeing and purging that bulimics engage in is extremely hard on the body. Stomach acid is incredibly corrosive. When tissues in the throat, mouth, and tongue are overexposed to the acid during purging, it can cause damage. Where the tongue meets the teeth, tooth enamel erosion often occurs. Calcium and vitamin D deficiencies lead to calcium loss in

Both anorexia and bulimia can dehydrate your body, making your face appear pale and highlighting dark circles under your eyes.

bones and teeth, and over time this causes gum disease and tooth loss. Constant vomiting and excessive laxative use also cause dehydration. Dehydration can cause dizziness and weakness, but more seriously it can lead to kidney failure, heart failure, and even death.

Continual forced vomiting can also seriously damage the esophagus. Esophageal reflux is a medical condition of the esophagus that causes partially digested food that is mixed with stomach acids to flow back up the esophagus. In addition to damaging the esophagus, the acids can also burn the larynx, causing chronic laryngitis. The condition can get so bad that food cannot be kept down and purging becomes an involuntary reaction. Reflux can also bring on a condition called Barrett's esophagus, which causes a change to the cells of the esophagus and is associated with esophagus cancer. Ripping the lining of the esophagus is another hazard of repetitive vomiting. These rips are called Mallory-Weiss tears, and they lead to throwing up blood. In some cases, the tears can be life threatening.

COMPLICATIONS FROM BINGE EATING

Unlike anorexia and bulimia, the health impacts of binge eating take longer to show up and affect an individual's overall health. Because binge eating is often associated with eating lots of carbohydrates and fat, patients have a tendency toward high blood pressure, type 2 diabetes, high cholesterol, gall bladder disease, and other digestive problems. The unhealthy eating behavior often leads to obesity, which in turn can cause joint and muscle pain. Binge

Foods high in carbohydrates, such as bread, cookies, and potato chips, are among the highest contributors to high blood pressure.

eating can also have a heavy psychological toll, and depression and suicidal thoughts are also common.

BLOOD PRESSURE AND BLOOD SUGAR

All types of eating disorders wreak havoc on blood pressure levels. Malnutrition and dehydration can cause low blood pressure, which in turn can cause irregular heartbeats. People with eating disorders can also experience an extreme and sudden drop in blood pressure when shifting from standing to sitting or lying down. This is called orthostatic hypotension, and symptoms include dizziness, blurred vision, pounding heart, headache, and even passing out. On the other extreme there is high blood pressure, or hypertension. This condition is most common in overeaters, and it can cause heart attacks, strokes, and kidney failure.

Blood sugar levels are also thrown out of whack when your body doesn't receive a balanced diet and appropriate caloric intake. Hypoglycemia is when blood glucose (sugar) levels drop below normal. This can occur from

EATING DISORDER DAMAGE

Eyes	blurred vision, glaucoma, blindness
Hair	brittle hair, head hair loss, lanugo
Teeth	tooth loss and gum disease
Esophagus	esophageal reflux, Mallory-Weiss tears, cell change associated with cancer
Heart	irregular heartbeats, thickening of heart muscle, heart attack, heart failure
Stomach	cramps, bloating, gastrointestinal bleeding, gastric rupture
Pancreas	pancreatitis, pancreas failure
Kidneys	infections and kidney failure
Joints and Bones	joint pain, low bone mass, osteoporosis
Muscles	muscle atrophy

hormonal or enzyme imbalances and can cause dizziness, confusion, and fainting. In extreme cases, it can lead to coma and death.

On the other end of the spectrum, eating disorders can also lead to type 2 diabetes. Diabetes is diagnosed when blood sugar levels are too high because the body is not producing insulin. The long-term potential complications of diabetes include eye problems, kidney disease, and nerve damage. People with diabetes are also twice as likely to develop heart disease.

ASK YOURSELF THIS

- *Why do you think Jennifer thought she looked good even though her clothes no longer fit her?*

- *If one of your friends started to show unusual symptoms like Jennifer's lanugo, what would you do, and why?*

- *The University of West England survey revealed that one in ten women would give up between two and five years of life in exchange for the ideal body. Would you give up years of your life in exchange for a different appearance?*

- *If you or one of your friends was living with an eating disorder, how do you think a celebrity admitting to the same problem would help?*

TESTS AND DIAGNOSIS

Daniel had always been the strong kid on his football team. His solid frame made him difficult to knock over, and he knew how to use it like a bulldozer to tackle. Everyone had always praised Daniel's defense skills on the field. And even though he knew he was

Admitting you have an unhealthy relationship with food and seeking help can be the most difficult steps in testing for and diagnosing an eating disorder.

eating more than he needed to, he told himself he should for football.

But that afternoon at practice, Daniel found out he wasn't going to be on the starting lineup for the first game of the season. He went home and went straight up to his room. In the evening, his mother called him to dinner, but he refused to join them. He blamed it on his mood and said he was just upset about practice. "What do I need a huge dinner for anymore?" he thought. "There's no need for me to bulk up this season."

The next morning after his mom left for work, Daniel skipped breakfast and school. He went back to school the next day, but his appetite had not returned, and he had no interest in socializing. He went straight home after school and went to bed. Daniel felt worthless. To him, he had lost the only thing he was good at.

After about a month of skipping meals and avoiding his friends, Daniel knew his mom was worried—and honestly, he kind of was, too. His normally thick, dark hair looked thinner and dull; and there was more of it on the bottom of the bathtub after he showered. He was extremely thin and pale, and the circles under his eyes made him look like he had been beaten up. His mom said she was taking him to the doctor this morning, and he decided he wouldn't fight her this time.

GETTING A DIAGNOSIS

Daniel's depression had snowballed into anorexia. It looked like Daniel was among what experts believe is a growing number of boys with eating disorders. Diagnosing an eating disorder can be very difficult. Patients and those closest to them often deny there is a problem. Some people self-diagnose a different health issue to justify eating less, eliminating foods, or losing weight. It is usually a loved one who has to convince the patient to seek help. Once the patient does seek help, it is usually necessary to see both a medical doctor and a mental health professional.

The most commonly used screening tests are the Eating Disorders Examination (EDE) and Eating Disorders Examination–Questionnaire

SLIPPING THROUGH THE CRACKS

Most people who have an eating disorder are going undiagnosed and untreated. The statistics show just how many people with an eating disorder are slipping through the cracks:

- Only 10 percent of people with eating disorders receive treatment.
- Only 35 percent of the people who receive treatment get it from a facility that specializes in eating disorders.
- Men are less likely to seek treatment than women.[1]

(EDE-Q). A doctor conducts the EDE, whereas the EDE-Q is a self-reported questionnaire. Both are considered valid ways to determine if a patient meets the specific criteria of an eating disorder. Mental health assessments are also an important part of diagnosing eating disorders. People with eating disorders often have other mental disorders, including depression, anxiety, or addiction to alcohol, illegal drugs, or prescription drugs.

The doctor will also do a physical examination, which includes measuring the patient's weight, height, and BMI. Checking blood pressure, heart rate, and temperature are also part of an initial screening test. Standard laboratory tests include a complete blood count,

SCOFF QUESTIONNAIRE

Medical professionals can use the SCOFF Questionnaire to determine if patients meet the full diagnostic criteria for anorexia or bulimia. The test consists of five questions, the key words of which create the acronym SCOFF. If you answer yes to two or more of the following questions, it is a fairly clear sign you have an eating disorder:

- "Do you make yourself sick because you feel uncomfortably full?
- Do you worry you have lost control over how much you eat?
- Have you recently lost more than one stone's worth of weight (14 pounds or 6.3 kg) in a three-month period?
- Do you believe yourself to be fat when others say you are too thin?
- Would you say that food dominates your life?"[2]

Both physical and mental health are evaluated when diagnosing an eating disorder.

as well as specific tests for electrolyte and protein levels. A urinalysis, thyroid screening, and liver and kidney tests are conducted. And finally, an electrocardiogram and bone density tests are done. The results of all these tests help to determine the acuteness of the disease, the damage that has been done, and the course of treatment.

MAKING A DIAGNOSIS

To be diagnosed with an eating disorder, a patient must meet the clinical criteria of the *DSM-5*. The most basic diagnostic criterion for bulimia that a doctor looks for is a pattern of bingeing and purging at least once a week for at least three months. For anorexia, the criteria include having low BMI, a refusal to maintain a body weight that is at or above the minimum normal weight for age and height, an intense fear of becoming fat even though the patient is underweight, and a distorted image of appearance or shape. Medical professionals must pay close attention because even though some patients may not meet all the criteria, there are often issues that still require medical intervention.

WHAT IS A HEALTHY WEIGHT?

The BMI calculation is the same for children, teens, and adults, but the criteria used to interpret the BMI number for children and teens are different from those used for adults. Percentiles based on sex are used to interpret the BMI of children and teens because body fat changes with age and differs between girls and boys. For adults, BMI is interpreted through categories that do not take into account sex or age. It is difficult to provide healthy weight ranges for children and teens because healthy weight ranges change with each month of age for each sex, as well as with height increases.

Eating until you are uncomfortably full and feeling ashamed of it are just two of the factors evaluated when diagnosing binge eating.

Binge eating is diagnosed when a patient has recurrent episodes of eating an abnormally large amount of food and feels a lack of control while doing so, when the patient binge eats at least once a week for at least three months, and if at least three of these factors are associated with their bingeing: eating rapidly, eating until uncomfortably full, eating large amounts when not hungry, eating alone out of embarrassment, or feeling disgusted, depressed, or guilty after eating.

FURTHER TESTING

If you have anorexia, further tests must be done if your weight has dropped to what doctors consider a dangerously low level. Your kidney function is tested, and an echocardiogram may also be done to check for damage to the heart, heart valves, and other heart structures. In cases

IT'S THE BRAIN

Results from a study conducted by a research team at the New York State Psychiatric Institute and the College of Physicians and Surgeons showed patients with bulimia appeared to have less impulse control when compared with healthy control patients. All the participants were given tasks that required them to overcome an impulsive response. The study concluded, "Self-regulatory processes are impaired in women with bulimia. . . . These findings enhance our understanding of . . . bulimia by pointing to abnormalities within a neural system . . . which may contribute to binge eating and other impulsive behaviors in women with bulimia."[3]

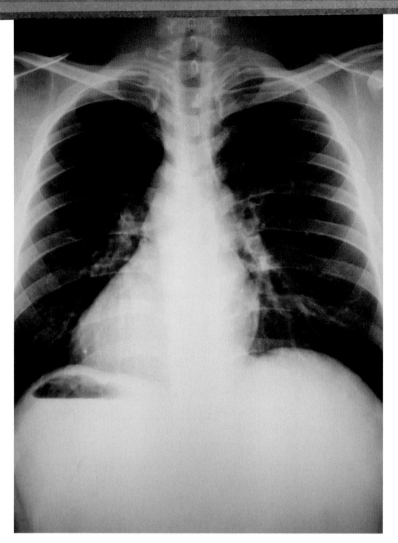

Doctors may take a chest X-ray to reveal whether you have come down with pneumonia due to anorexia.

where body weight is even more extremely low, or when it has remained below ideal body weight (IBW) for more than six months, doctors will also assess immune function and bone mineral density.

ASK YOURSELF THIS

- *Why do you think Daniel, similar to so many people with an eating disorder, could not admit to his mother he had stopped eating and might have a problem?*

- *Do you think it would have made a difference if Daniel had told someone he felt as though he had lost the only thing he was good at? How so?*

- *Statistics show that men are less likely than women to seek treatment for an eating disorder. Why do you think this is?*

- *If you thought a friend was looking skinny and unhealthy, what would compel you or prevent you from saying something to your friend or someone close to your friend?*

- *How do you think learning about healthy food and exercise choices at a younger age would make a difference in society's attitude about food and body image?*

TREATMENT

t was the night of senior prom, and instead of dancing with her friends, Aaliyah was in the hospital with her doctor and parents. Aaliyah had taken her weight loss to a problematic extreme while trying to lose weight for her prom night, and this past week, her parents had taken

her to the hospital. Aaliyah refused to accept
it, but the doctors confirmed it: Aaliyah was
diagnosed with anorexia.

By the time her parents took her to get
help, doctors felt admission to the hospital was
necessary to increase her body weight and
improve her health and psychological state.
Aaliyah's parents were brought in to discuss and
develop a nutrition plan for her.

Dr. Ventura began with a nutritional
assessment to help determine any biochemical
imbalances that needed to be addressed before
focusing on Aaliyah's weight gain. Afterward,
Aaliyah's parents were able to ask about
Aaliyah's meal plan.

"So how big of meals should we be
preparing for her after she comes home?" asked
Aaliyah's mom. Aaliyah felt as if she were a
baby, learning to eat for the first time. She knew
they wanted her to eat more, but she wasn't
sure she was ready to do it. She still hadn't lost
all the weight she wanted to fit into her prom
dress. Aaliyah sat and listened while Dr. Ventura
told her parents about her new meal plan.

"We'll encourage Aaliyah to begin by eating
very small amounts of food. We'll increase
that intake very gradually over time," said
Dr. Ventura.

"How many meals will I have to eat?" Aaliyah finally asked after several minutes of silence.

"Your meals will be scheduled for set times, and you'll need to eat three balanced meals each day—no meal skipping," Dr. Ventura said.

"But what if I'm not hungry?" Aaliyah protested.

"Our goal is for you to gain between one and two pounds (0.45–0.9 kg) per week, but not more," Dr. Ventura responded. "It will take some time, but we'll get you back to healthy, Aaliyah."

Aaliyah's family and treatment team knew they had a long battle in front of them.

MULTIFACETED TREATMENT

Treating eating disorders is multifaceted. The primary focus for health-care professionals is usually restoring health. It has also been found that a multidisciplinary approach to therapy is more effective than psychological counseling alone. A support team can be made up of any combination of eating disorder professionals, including medical doctors, nurses, dieticians, and various types of mental health therapists. If you are diagnosed with an eating disorder, you may go through a combination of treatments. In addition to stabilizing healthy eating habits, your doctor may also suggest psychotherapy and medications for treatment and recovery.

Treatment varies from patient to patient and depends on which eating disorder you suffer from. Many factors are taken into account when deciding what the best type of treatment is and what level of care is required. Your physical condition, psychological state, behavior, family support system, and weight are all considered.

ANOREXIA TREATMENT

Because patients with anorexia are often in denial, they are usually in pretty bad shape by the time they seek help and start treatment. For this reason, treatment usually begins by focusing on regaining health, whether it is gaining weight, ending the cycle of starvation, or restoring nutrient levels. It will be impossible to address psychological recovery if your body is not functioning properly or if your life is in danger.

UNHEALTHY DIETING PRACTICES COMMON IN COLLEGE-AGED WOMEN

A 2006 study published online in the *Nutrition Journal* found that 83 percent of the 185 college participants surveyed used dieting for weight loss. However, the methods they were using were ineffective, unhealthy, or dangerous. Although many of the dieters said they exercised to lose weight, most were not doing enough physical activity to do so. Researchers also found two troubling behaviors: 32 percent of participants skipped breakfast to lose weight, and 9 percent smoked cigarettes.[1]

During cognitive behavioral therapy, your therapist will help you change negative thoughts you have about your appearance.

At the same time it must be decided what kind of psychotherapy is best for you. There are many different options. Cognitive behavioral therapy (CBT) is one of the more common approaches. This approach is based on the idea that people's emotions are controlled by their opinions and views of the world. The therapist will work with you to change negative thought patterns and belief systems, with the idea that you can learn to control your thinking and behavior. Other types of therapy may include family-based therapy or psychoanalysis, which is based on the idea that individuals are often unaware of the things that are controlling their emotions and behavior. Psychoanalytic treatment explores how these unconscious factors affect relationships, thought patterns, emotion, and behavior.

No medications have been proven to be effective in treating anorexia, but if you also have depression or an anxiety disorder also exists, your doctor might prescribe medication to treat these disorders. It is important to ask a therapist what the orientation of his or her specific program is so you know what you are getting into.

THE MAUDSLEY APPROACH TO TREATING ANOREXIA

A popular hands-on approach for treating adolescents with anorexia, particularly those who have had an eating disorder for less than three years, is the Maudsley approach. The Maudsley approach believes family plays an essential role in the successful treatment of anorexia. Most therapeutic interventions focus on the individual and not on the family involved. The Maudsley approach is an intensive at-home program in which parents play an active and positive role in restoring their child's weight, handing the control of eating back over to the adolescent and encouraging normal adolescent

In treatments such as the Maudsley approach, it has been shown that family interaction and support can help aid in anorexia treatment.

development. The approach has proved to be relatively successful. Studies have shown that approximately two-thirds of adolescent anorexia patients have recovered at the end of their family-based therapy, and 75 to 90 percent have recovered their full weight five years later. Better yet, most patients required no more than 20 treatment sessions over a six- to 12-month period, and 80 percent of patients were back to an appropriate weight by this time as well.[2]

TREATING BULIMIA

Unlike anorexia, antidepressants have proven effective in treating bulimia. It is for this reason patients with bulimia are commonly treated with a combination of psychotherapy and antidepressants. The only antidepressant specifically approved by the Food and Drug Administration (FDA) to treat bulimia is fluoxetine, more commonly known by the brand name Prozac.

Psychotherapy for bulimics may include CBT, family-based treatment, or dialectical behavior therapy, which helps patients learn behavioral skills to better tolerate stress and regulate their emotions. Interpersonal therapy (IPT) may also be used. The goal of IPT is for patients to identify

HARDWIRED FOR BULIMIA

A psychologist at the Oregon Research Institute examined brain activity in 33 female adolescents and 43 women after they tasted a chocolate milkshake. He found that over a one-year period, participants who showed more activation of key regions in the brain associated with rewards reported an increase in bulimic behavior. Researchers believe this study shows that "if children are exposed to a high-fat, high-sugar diet early in development, they develop a strong preference for and craving for these foods that doesn't otherwise emerge, and that this is what sets people up for bulimia."[3]

and change interpersonal problems, or problems they're having interacting with others. Depending on where you land on the weight scale, underweight or overweight, dieticians will also work with you to develop an eating plan that restores healthy habits and a healthy relationship with food.

TREATING BINGE EATING

Unlike when treating anorexia and bulimia, restoring emotional well-being takes priority over restoring physical health when treating binge eaters. Binge eating is often associated with other mental health disorders, such as depression and anxiety, as well as an inability to manage emotions. One study reported that anger was the emotion most often reported before an eating binge. Feelings of loneliness, shame, disgust, or exhaustion had the highest probability of leading to binge eating behavior.

Treatment includes psychotherapy that focuses on learning to cope with negative thought patterns, improving interpersonal relationships, and developing new strategies for managing stress. If weight loss is also necessary, it is not usually addressed until after the patient is emotionally stable and the binge eating is under control. In some cases, antidepressant medication may be prescribed, but a recent study showed medication can actually do harm. The FDA warns that anyone taking antidepressants should be closely monitored by a medical professional. Possible side effects include worsening depression, suicidal thoughts or behavior, trouble sleeping, social withdrawal, and general agitation.

On the other hand, CBT has been shown to reduce binge eating for up to four months after treatment, but it was not associated with weight loss.

TREATMENT CENTERS AND HOSPITALIZATION

How and where treatment is given depends on a number of factors, including how motivated you are to get well, your medical condition and psychological state, what kind of support system

COSTLY TREATMENT

According to Mirasol Eating Disorder Recovery Centers, only one in ten people with eating disorders receive treatment. Of those, approximately 80 percent do not get the intensity of treatment they need, often leaving the treatment center weeks earlier than recommended.[4] One reason for this could be the cost of treatment. In a survey of 109 eating disorder specialists around the United States, nearly all of them—96.7 percent—believe their patients with anorexia nervosa are put in life-threatening situations because of early discharge mandated by health insurance companies that refuse to pay for further treatment. And a full 100 percent of these specialists believe some of their patients have had relapses due to limitations of care.[5]

you have, and how well you are functioning in social, school, and work environments. Treatment availability and health insurance will also be considered. Once all these factors are analyzed, eating disorder care can range from outpatient treatment to acute care hospitalization.

Outpatient treatment is structured to individual needs and is very intensive. It can include group therapy sessions and meetings with members of a treatment team, including nutritionists, physicians, and psychotherapists. Treatment can last for weeks, months, or even years for some anorexia patients.

Hospital care can range from partial hospitalization for up to eight hours a day to inpatient services in which the patient needs more focused, 24-hour supervision and support. Acute care is required if the patient's medical condition has deteriorated to the point that his or her safety is at risk. Dehydration, electrolyte imbalance, extremely low

ABUSING TREATMENT

One issue that can arise when someone with an eating disorder is admitted to a treatment facility or joins group therapy is competitiveness. Being around other people with eating disorders may trigger a desire to be the thinnest in the group, or the patient may take advantage of the situation to get tips on how to lose weight or trick the scales at weigh-in.

body weight, low blood pressure, and low body temperature are all reasons medical professionals may admit a patient to the hospital.

ASK YOURSELF THIS

- *Why do you think most people with eating disorders develop them before they are 20 years old?*

- *Why do you think cognitive behavior therapy has proven to be one of the more effective ways of treating people with eating disorders?*

- *Do any of your friends struggle with being overweight and poor body image? What are some things you can do to help them feel satisfied with how they look and feel?*

- *The Maudsley approach encourages families to be involved with the patient's treatment and therapy. If you have been diagnosed with anorexia, what benefit would you see in your family's involvement?*

HOME AND LIFESTYLE CHANGES

"**F**ee, fi, fo, fum, see Kelly the giant run!" Kelly could still hear the taunts from her last day of recess in middle school. All the other girls in her class had pointed at her and laughed as they sang the rhyme. And Kelly had just kept running.

If your current treatment isn't working for you,
talk to your doctor about alternative options, such
adventure-based therapy.

She ran all the way home and devoured an entire package of cookies. She was angry with the girls who teased her, embarrassed by her body, and ashamed she had just eaten so many cookies. That was Kelly's first binge, but it soon became an unhealthy coping mechanism. Kelly's parents realized she had a problem when they discovered an overflowing garbage bag of candy wrappers stuffed in the back of her closet.

After finding out Kelly's secret, Kelly's parents immediately stepped in to help. She participated in the usual treatments, including CBT and medication for her depression, but nothing seemed to help. Her family decided to look into alternative therapies for Kelly. They decided to try adventure-based therapy (ABT). This past summer, Kelly participated in ABT activities with other eating disorder patients that taught her problem-solving skills and independence. She went on overnight camping trips with other girls her age where they had to work together to set up camp and build fires. The girls also went on long, physically challenging nature hikes. She learned that her height and strength sometimes had its advantages, which improved her self-esteem. Kelly also learned how to ask for help, as well as how to offer it. And she learned it was okay to fail sometimes. It didn't mean it was the end of the world. ABT combined with CBT taught Kelly to manage her emotions, stress, and anxiety in healthier ways than bingeing.

A LITTLE ADVENTURE MAY HELP

Mirasol Eating Disorder Recovery Center director Diane Ryan introduced ABT to the center in 2006, and they have seen encouraging results. EEG brain maps and psychological tests showed a significant decrease in symptoms of anxiety and depression.[1] Clients were given the Children's Depression Inventory (CDI) and Coping Skills Inventory (CSI) both before and after their adventure camping trips. Most clients reported a decrease in symptoms of stress and an increase in their ability to cope with stress after ABT.

INTEGRATING ALTERNATIVE TREATMENTS

Kelly was lucky she had supportive parents who were willing to try alternative therapies to help her. All experts agree an eating disorder of any kind and of any severity is not something that should be managed alone. After admitting there is a problem and treatment has started, it is important for patients to stay on track in all areas of their lives. Alternative therapies and the right lifestyle approach can help.

ALTERNATIVE THERAPIES

Most health professionals now agree combining physical medicine with psychology and alternative therapy is the best way to address many medical and mental health issues. Alternative therapies now play important roles in many patients' treatment plans. Massage and therapeutic touch have been shown to help reduce anxiety, which is often associated with eating disorders. Acupuncture is also believed to help relieve anxiety and stress and has also proved to help those with digestive problems and food cravings. Meditation, yoga, and hypnosis can also better connect you with your

ANIMAL-ASSISTED THERAPY

Animals have been used for all kinds of therapeutic reasons, and the benefits of having a four-legged companion have long been reported. One study showed that after 20 minutes with a therapy dog, people had a drop in stress hormones such as cortisol and adrenaline and an increase in positive and social hormones such as oxytocin, dopamine, and endorphins.[2] Equine therapy can also help people develop more self-acceptance. It combines learning the skills of caring for a horse with developing psychosocial skills through positive interaction with the horse. Research has suggested equine therapy can help people improve nurturing abilities, self-confidence, communication skills, and the ability to be in the moment.

Research has shown interaction with a pet, such as a dog, can release the "happy" hormones endorphins and dopamine.

body and assist you in becoming more sensitive to its cues about eating, hunger, and fullness.

ABT and animal-based therapy have both been effective in treating eating disorders. ABT can include challenge courses and extended wilderness trips. It puts patients in an unfamiliar adventure setting that includes emotional and physical challenges. Participants are also often required to solve problems as a group. The patient learns to use stress in a positive way by focusing on achievement and success rather than an eating disorder. Research has shown that after ABT, patients showed fewer perfectionist tendencies and reported feeling more connected with their bodies.

HERBAL REMEDIES

You should be cautious of herbs and natural remedies. Many herbs can interact with medications and can have serious side effects. It is also easy for someone with an eating disorder to start abusing dietary supplements that are designed to suppress appetite or stimulate weight loss. Natural remedies, herbs, or dietary supplements should not be taken without first consulting a medical doctor. Vitamin and mineral supplements, such as vitamin D and calcium, are sometimes prescribed by doctors to help with nutrition deficiencies.

MINERAL AND VITAMIN DEFICIENCIES

Since as early as the 1970s, researchers have been looking at the connection between a zinc deficiency and the onset of anorexia. A zinc deficiency can show up as depression, amenorrhea, loss of appetite, and weight loss. Other studies have shown that people with self-harm behavior had low plasma essential fatty acids (EFA) levels and low cholesterol concentrations. Symptoms of vitamin B deficiency also overlap with symptoms of anorexia including weakness, tiredness, or light-headedness; rapid heartbeat and breathing; pale skin; diarrhea or constipation; and weight loss. Further research into nutrition therapy could hold more keys to both treating and preventing anorexia and other eating disorders.

Make hanging out with friends a part of your self-care plan. Engaging in activities with others can help take your mind off of old habits.

SELF-CARE: HAVING A PLAN AND KEEPING IT

To recover from your eating disorder, it is important to stick with your plan and not skip therapy sessions. You must adhere to your meal plans and take all supplements and medications prescribed. It also helps to be educated about eating disorders. Understanding the condition you are living with empowers you and helps you feel control over your eating disorder and recovery.

Learning to be kind to yourself will also go a long way in helping to break the pattern of negative and damaging thinking. You should avoid weighing yourself and dieting unless your medical team has instructed you to do so. You should also resist the temptation to look in the mirror, as this could trigger eating disorder behaviors. Engaging in appropriate physical activities that focus on having fun and being healthy—instead of weight loss—is also a good idea.

Avoiding isolation and developing normal social relationships will also help in the recovery process. Reaching out to family and accepting their love and support is healthy. Meeting friends after school or joining a club can also be a good way of breaking old routines that could trigger eating disorder behavior.

ASK YOURSELF THIS

- *What therapies would you ask your doctor about if the medical treatment you were receiving for your eating disorder wasn't working? Why?*

- *How do you think Kelly's life would be different if she did not use ABT?*

- *Why do you think ABT is proving to be an effective way of treating eating disorders?*

- *Do you have a self-care plan? What habits have you changed to adhere to your plan?*

7

COPING AND SUPPORT

Shawna had a tough decision to make: continue seeing her friends and risk having a relapse of bulimia, or cut them out of her life until she felt stronger. Listening to them talk at lunch today had made her realize all they did was criticize others. Everything

When attempting to treat and cope with your eating disorder, it's important to surround yourself with supportive and understanding people.

they said focused on weight, appearance, and fashion. Therapy had helped Shawna realize she wasn't overweight. But she still found it difficult to listen to her thinner friends talk about how fat they were or say another person in school was fat.

One night after school Shawna talked to her mom about her friends. "They're just always so judgmental. After therapy, I feel fine about myself. I actually like the way I look. But when I hear them say things about every other person's appearance, I can't help but think they're judging me, too."

"You may not want to hear it," Shawna's mom replied, "but I think it's time to spend time with other friends."

"But I've been friends with them since elementary school. Where am I supposed to find new friends now?"

"What about Christine from choir? You two used to have so much fun together. Maybe you should get back into that," Shawna's mom suggested.

Shawna decided to pursue an old hobby and join the choir. Her friendship with Christine started up again, and soon she was able to trust and confide in her. She started eating lunch with Christine and other girls from choir who were more sensitive and supportive of her situation. She hoped someday she'd be able to enjoy the company of her old friends without feeling down about herself. But until then, she understood that surrounding herself with the right support system would speed up her recovery and help prevent her from falling back into bulimia.

PRO ANA WEB SITES

There are Web sites that actually glorify anorexia and bulimia. Called pro ana (pro anorexia), pro mia (pro bulimia), or thinspo (thin inspiration) sites, these Web sites and blogs provide people with "thinspiration"— information on how to get and stay extremely thin. They present anorexia and bulimia as acceptable lifestyle choices. Many of the sites claim they are not pro ana or pro mia, but they often focus on photos of extremely thin girls and women, include tips on anorexic dieting, and give hints on how to hide the behavior from friends and family. For anyone at risk of developing an eating disorder or in treatment for one, these Web sites are incredibly dangerous.

COPING IN ALL AREAS OF LIFE

The biggest obstacle to overcoming and recovering from an eating disorder is admitting to having one. Once you have admitted to having a problem, coping is essential to recovery. It is important to try to shut out the mixed messages the media and others may be sending. Society tends to

Avoid weighing yourself. Instead, focus on being comfortable and accepting yourself the way you are.

associate thinness with success and beauty, and it is difficult not to buy into this.

To help improve body image, all experts suggest putting away the scale. Other ideas include wearing comfortable clothes, starting the morning with good grooming, walking proud, and being comfortable and familiar with your body. Coping strategies for dealing with food and eating can include changing the subject when other people talk about food, weight, or body size and shape; setting an eating routine that includes three well-balanced meals; eating with people who do not bug you about eating; developing a support system for times when eating has been a problem; making a date to eat with someone; avoiding bathrooms after meals; and making sure to enjoy more about a meal than just the food.

To control and cope with urges to binge, try keeping busy. Work on a hobby, go for a walk, watch a movie, talk with someone supportive, or listen to music. If you do slip up and binge, forgive yourself, remove yourself from your eating place, and get yourself back on track with routine

12-STEP PROGRAMS

One method to help with coping is to join a 12-step program. Most people associate 12-step programs with alcoholics, but over the years this kind of support group has popped up for all kinds of addictions. Eating Disorders Anonymous (EDA) is one of them. Built on the same philosophy as Alcoholics Anonymous— that accountability to others aids in recovery— the only requirement for membership is a desire to recover from an eating disorder. Meetings are open and nonjudgmental, and members are encouraged to share phone numbers and contact information so they can call for support when needed. EDA was founded in 2000 and holds meetings in 40 states and nine different countries.

eating. You also need to be able to identify problem situations that are likely to trigger thoughts or behavior that may contribute to your eating disorder behaviors so you can have a plan in place before a problem occurs.

COPING WITH LONELINESS AND LOW SELF-CONFIDENCE

Feelings of loneliness and isolation are common. To deal with these feelings, try doing things that involve other people, such as volunteering, joining a club, or even just making eye contact with people around you. At the same time, it is important to learn to hold your own. Say what you need to and insist on your rights. When things are not going well, do not assume it is all your fault. Clarify your own feelings and choose if you want to act on them.

When it comes to coping, remember that you may not always be the best judge of whether you're eating enough or are at a healthy weight. Look for positive role models and remind yourself that superthin celebrities don't represent healthy bodies. It is important to surround yourself with the right people to ensure you are receiving supportive messages. Keep a list of people you can call to help you through the tough times. And don't hesitate to call a member of your treatment team so you

Surround yourself with positive friends and keep busy. The social interaction and physical activity can keep you away from eating disorder triggers.

can address any specific issue you are having problems coping with.

ASK YOURSELF THIS

- *What do you think might have happened to Shawna if she continued socializing regularly with her old group of friends while she was still struggling with recovery?*

- *If you were struggling with an eating disorder, what kinds of activities would you consider doing to keep busy and on track for recovery? How and why do you think they would help?*

- *What kinds of things do you and your friends talk about when you are together? Do you find the conversation often focuses on how people look? How does that make you feel?*

- *What positive things may Shawna gain from her illness and recovery?*

- *Some people think it is wrong for corporations such as Instagram and Tumblr to ban pro ana Web sites and posts because it infringes on freedom of speech. Do you agree or disagree? Why?*

A NURSE'S GUIDE TO COPING

The University of Wisconsin has produced a list of coping strategies written by a group of nurses who work with people who have eating disorders. These are just guidelines, but the suggestions are in line with recommendations in eating disorder reference manuals and support guides. They have broken the coping strategies into ten main categories:

- Improve body image
- Cope with eating
- Control urges to binge
- Deal with feelings after a binge
- Improve self-esteem
- Tell yourself you are okay
- Nurture and reward yourself
- Deal with feeling isolated
- Deal with tension
- Hold your own assertively[1]

8

HELPING SOMEONE ELSE: REACHING OUT

"Isaac, you weren't listening to me again. What's wrong with you?" Sarah almost screamed at Isaac. She was worried about him. They had been friends since they were babies. But recently Sarah had noticed Isaac wasn't as talkative when they were together—and that hadn't been as often as usual lately. Today was the first time they had hung out in almost a month.

Sarah stared at Isaac. "I said, you aren't eating again. Why not?"

"I'm not hungry. Why do you bug me so much? I gotta go." Isaac stood up and left. This was something else that was new. He was much more short-tempered than usual. This was not the first time Sarah had noticed Isaac wasn't eating. He had turned down more trips to the mall food court or ice cream parlor than Sarah could count. Or when they did go, he would say he wasn't hungry anymore as they were ordering. Sarah noticed he had been losing weight. She knew something was wrong, but she didn't know what or how to find out.

Sarah decided to talk to her parents. "Something's up with Isaac. He never seems to eat. I can tell he's losing weight, but when I talk about food he gets really defensive. I don't know what to say to him anymore."

"I'm no doctor, but it sounds like Isaac is having some serious issues with eating," her father said.

"Yes, I think you should talk to the counselor or doctor at school. They'll be able to get him the help he needs. Isaac won't even have to

know it was you who mentioned something,"
Sarah's mom chimed in.

It wasn't easy for her to go to the counselor.
She felt like she was betraying Isaac, but
she knew the counselor would be able to
recommend resources and contact Isaac's
parents.

STARTING THE CONVERSATION

Reaching out to someone you think may be in
trouble is never easy. But if a friend or relative
has an eating disorder, it is important he or
she gets help. The first thing you should do
is educate yourself about the various eating
disorders. Informing yourself will help ensure
you don't say or do the wrong thing. You should
also prepare a list of resources to offer if you
are asked.

WHAT NOT TO SAY

It is important that family and friends of someone with an
eating disorder remember to keep their words supportive
and thoughtful of his or her feelings. For example, don't
comment on what your family member or friend eats. For
people with eating disorders, eating in front of others
can be very difficult. They may think everyone is paying
attention to what they're eating, and if you comment on
it, they may not want to eat. Don't beg them to eat—doing
this may also push them even further away from eating
and make them more self-conscious. Also, try not to
comment on their appearance. This signals that you're
watching their appearance and possibly judging them.
Instead, ask how they are feeling.

When first approaching someone you think may have an eating disorder, you must be prepared for the person to deny there is a problem; this is a common response. Be careful not to use the knowledge you have gained about eating disorders to talk down to, nag, or scare the person. It is important to listen without judging.

The National Eating Disorders Association offers some suggestions in their parent tool kit on how to start a conversation with a loved one. Make sure you plan to have your discussion in a private place where you will not be interrupted. Express your concerns in a calm, caring, and compassionate way. Do not focus on weight, food, or exercise, but do pinpoint specific actions or behaviors you have noticed that concern you.

SUPPORT FOR FAMILY MEMBERS

Eating disorders can be very hard on the family and friends of the victim. Everyone impacted by the eating disorder needs support. Patient treatment often involves family counseling, but there are also networks that serve as good resource and support centers for those closest to the patient. The National Eating Disorders Association has the Parent, Family & Friends Network, which publishes a magazine, offers webinars, and connects those in need of support with highly trained volunteers who have supported their own loved ones.

If your friend continues denying the problem, take a break from the conversation but promise to revisit the subject.

Share any observations you have made about your loved one's mood, health, or relationships. Ask if he or she is willing to consider the possibility that something is wrong or is willing to talk to a health-care professional about your concerns.

If the person continues denying an eating disorder, don't get frustrated. Even if the person doesn't admit to a problem right away, at least you have let him or her know you are concerned and you are there to offer support if it is needed. Control is often a big issue for people with eating disorders. It is impossible to force someone to acknowledge a problem or accept help. Always try and be a good role model, but no matter the outcome, it is important not to let your loved one's eating disorder rule your life. Make sure to take care of yourself; both stress and lack of sleep can lead to your own health problems.

SUPPORT DURING AND AFTER TREATMENT

Once your loved one has acknowledged a problem, there are a number of ways to be supportive. Ask what you can do to help, but don't hover or judge. Be patient and talk to the person in a kind voice even if you are angry or upset. Understand the person is not seeking attention or pity. Have compassion and listen openly when the person wants to talk. Remind your loved one you only want what is best for him or her and that he or she has

SLOW TO RECOVER

Family and friends must remember recovery is not quick. Patient outcome studies for patients five and ten years after receiving treatment show recovery from an eating disorder is slow and not guaranteed. Approximately half of patients recover, one-quarter improve but still have residual symptoms, and one-quarter remain ill or die.[1]

lots of people who care. Compliment things about the person that don't focus on physical appearance: talent, success, sense of humor, or personality. Encourage all treatment and activities recommended by the care team, such as keeping appointments, taking medications, and sticking to meal plans. Encourage social activities that don't involve food or shopping for clothes. But most important, remain patient; recovery takes time, and food and eating may always be an issue for your loved one.

ASK YOURSELF THIS

- *If you were in Sarah's position, who would you turn to and why?*

- *How do you think having Sarah participate in Isaac's treatment and therapy may benefit Isaac?*

- *How do you think using the services of a support group or hotline would benefit someone with an eating disorder or someone close to a person with an eating disorder?*

- *In what ways can you imagine Isaac's eating disorder having negative effects on his parents?*

9

PREVENTION

Grace had always remembered her mother describing her as a little turkey when she was born; all round and chubby. And as she grew older, she stayed that way. She was never really overweight, but people often used expressions like "solid build" or "baby fat" to describe her. She was always heavier and shorter than her sister. One day after school last year, she had come home and told her mom, "I'm fat. The girls at school even said so!" That was the day Grace's mother decided to throw away the scale at home.

It was now her senior year, and she felt much more secure with her body image. Over the past year, Grace's mother had taught her and her sisters to focus on a balanced, nutritional diet and healthy exercise—not weight or body shape and size. Conversations around the family dinner table centered on healthy food choices, why variety in exercise was important, and the long-term negative health impacts of excessive weight. Tonight, Grace's mom taught them how to make homemade salsa.

"Why don't you three go grab some tomatoes, jalapeños, and cilantro from the garden," Grace's mom told Grace and her sisters. "I'm teaching you how to make your grandma's secret salsa recipe tonight."

Grace was thankful for her mom's tips. Teaching her to cook and eat healthy foods made her feel so much better about her bigger build. "Yeah, I may be built a little bit bigger than the other girls, but I'm being healthy," she told herself.

PREVENTION FROM A VARIETY OF SOURCES

Grace's mom did a great job of preventing potential eating disorders in her daughters— especially Grace, who was already worried about her appearance. She taught them the importance of healthy lifestyle choices. Because multiple factors can lead to acquiring an eating disorder, eating disorders are not always preventable. Fortunately, there are things that can be done to aid in prevention. Parents, teachers, and coaches can all contribute to helping children and young adults have healthy attitudes about food, eating, and exercise. The messages

SELF-ESTEEM MATTERS

In 2008, clinical psychologist and eating disorder specialist Ann Kearney-Cooke collaborated with the Dove Self-Esteem Fund to gauge girls' self-esteem. They interviewed 3,344 girls ages 8 to 17 in 20 major US cities. The results paint a clear picture of the importance of good self-esteem. Seventy-five percent of girls with low self-esteem reported engaging in negative behavior such as self-harm, smoking, and bullying when they were feeling bad about themselves, compared with only 25 percent of girls with high self-esteem. Twenty-five percent of girls with low self-esteem report disordered eating, compared to 7 percent of girls with high self-esteem. And more than 34 percent of girls with low self-esteem think they are not good enough daughters.[1]

children and young adults receive do make a difference. And researchers have also found a number of prevention programs to be successful in reducing the risk of the onset of an eating disorder. Prevention begins with education.

EDUCATION AND COMMUNICATION

Taking the time to learn about eating disorders can go a long way toward preventing an issue in the future. Understanding the messages, situations, and stressors that may trigger an eating disorder is a good first step. Learning about healthy eating and lifestyle choices will also help you avoid making bad choices or judgments. And knowing that thin does not equate to beauty, health, or success will help improve self-image.

Studies have shown that most individuals with eating disorders also suffer from low self-esteem. Having good self-esteem and self-respect are important preventative measures against eating disorders. To have good self-esteem means to be generally satisfied with yourself and your accomplishments. Having a positive outlook on life, setting realistic goals, and feeling valued and loved are also all part of good self-esteem. Building strong family relationships and solid honest friendships, having a safe and secure

Educate yourself on eating disorder facts, triggers, and solutions to set you on the path for a healthier future.

home to live in, and finding hobbies you enjoy and are good at will all go a long way to building self-esteem.

Your attitude about and relationship with food also make a difference. Talk to your family, and make it a point to get out and get active together. Have conversations about the genetic reasons why there is such diversity in body shapes and sizes, and talk about why it is wrong to pass judgment on people based on their physical appearance. Learn about the dangers of trying to change your body size and shape through dieting. Remind your family members you think they are beautiful for their individuality. And make mealtime an adventure by trying new foods and cooking together.

CARELESS COMMENTS

It is difficult to fight a battle of prevention when icons in the fashion industry still make light of the problem. In 2009, supermodel Kate Moss made the careless comment, "Nothing tastes as good as skinny feels."[2]

PREVENTION PROGRAMS

A number of eating disorder prevention programs have popped up over the years with varying degrees of success. The Body Project is an interactive four, six, or eight-session intervention aimed at getting girls to take an active stand against the thin ideal. Students publicly discuss and critique the thin ideal with the idea being that if they argue against an idea, they are less likely to subscribe to it. The Body Project has proven successful at reducing people's risk of developing both eating disorder symptoms and obesity. Results suggest that for every 100 young women who complete the intervention, approximately nine fewer should develop eating issues.[3]

The Healthy Weight intervention is another prevention program that has had positive results. Studies found it reduced future eating disorder symptoms and obesity in participants, improved social functioning, and reduced health care use. It is different from other programs in that it encourages healthy weight through gradual changes to diet and exercise. The program also uses motivational interviewing and public commitments to motivate patients.

Weigh to Eat is a school-based program that focuses on changing attitudes and behaviors toward nutrition, weight control, and body and self-image. This program has been particularly effective in improving knowledge about binge eating. Overall, it has been found that interventions that worked to decrease risk factors and promote healthy weight control behaviors were most effective.

Keep family and friends close, and focus on enjoying your life!

A STEP FORWARD

There are a number of actions you, your family, and your friends can take part in together to help make sure you have a healthy relationship with food and your body, but remember you must be willing to take a step forward. Admitting you have an unhealthy relationship with food is the first step in tackling your eating disorder. Know that taking care of your body is important, and you are not alone in your battle.

IS OBESITY PREVENTION CAUSING EATING DISORDERS?

Eating disorder organizations believe the school-based programs that focus on weight in the current "war against obesity" are having an effect opposite to the one intended. The Eating Disorders Coalition is so concerned they wrote a letter to First Lady Michelle Obama asking her to rethink her childhood obesity campaign, Let's Move, which focuses on fighting obesity and instilling healthy behaviors in US children. The letter states, "The well-intentioned, but under informed and unproven strategy of focusing on weight fuels weight-prejudice and neglects groups which may be in equal need of improving their health and lifestyle. There is also the concern that these programs may contribute to negative self-esteem, body dissatisfaction, and eating disordered behaviors. Weight alone does not provide the full picture regarding health status; consideration of lifestyle, activity patterns, and physical and mental health measures are extremely important. Further, assuming illness based on weight alone, without proven cause and effect, may lead to harmful and discriminatory practices."[4]

ASK YOURSELF THIS

- *How do you imagine Grace would be different if her mother had started putting her on diets when she was a child?*

- *What negative behaviors do you think having a scale in the home can lead to?*

- *Have you ever had feelings of low self-esteem? What did you or could you do to feel better about yourself?*

- *The Healthy Weight intervention encourages public commitments to change. How do you think this helps in prevention?*

JUST THE FACTS

The *Diagnostic and Statistical Manual of Mental Disorders*, Fifth Edition (*DSM-5*) defines anorexia nervosa, bulimia, avoidant/restrictive food intake disorder, and binge eating as eating disorders.

Feeding and eating conditions not elsewhere classified (FEC NEC) are eating-related disorders that do not match the diagnostic criteria of anorexia, bulimia, avoidant/restrictive food intake disorder, or binge eating. These include orthorexia and anorexia athletica.

Behaviors that are characteristic of someone with anorexia include restricting calories, obsessively measuring portions, only eating specific foods, and skipping entire meals on a daily basis for an extended period of time.

An individual is diagnosed as anorexic if he or she has a distorted body image, a fear of becoming fat, and diets excessively to the point of severe weight loss.

People who suffer from bulimia engage in a cyclical pattern of eating large amounts of food followed by immediate purging, frequently by forced vomiting.

The *DSM-5* defines binge eating as "recurring episodes of eating significantly more food in a short period of time than most people would eat under similar circumstances, with episodes marked by feelings of lack of control." The behavior must occur at least once a week for a period of three months for a person to be clinically diagnosed as a binge eater.

Ten to 15 percent of people with anorexia or bulimia, and 40 percent of diagnosed binge eaters, are males.

Eighty-six percent of people with eating disorders reported onset by the time they were 20 years old.

Research has shown that in sports in which participants are judged and scored there is a 13 percent prevalence of eating disorders, versus only 3 percent in refereed sports. Elite female athletes show an even higher tendency toward eating disorders at 20 percent, compared with 9 percent in the control group.

Eating disorders have the highest mortality rate of all mental illnesses.

WHERE TO TURN

If You Think You Have a Problem

If you think you have an unhealthy relationship with food and may have an eating disorder, the National Eating Disorders Association (NEDA) and Mental Health Screening partnered to develop a free anonymous self-assessment to help determine risk of an eating disorder and whether clinical intervention is needed. Visit www.MyBodyScreening.org.

If You Think a Friend Has a Problem

NEDA offers a number of supports including a hotline, as well as "click to chat," where you can text message with a Helpline volunteer instead of speaking with one on the phone. NEDA also offers NEDA Navigators, trained volunteers who have experience dealing with the diagnosis and treatment of eating disorders. They are available to offer informal support, knowledge, and guidance to those who don't know where to turn. Visit www.nationaleatingdisorders.org/neda-navigators.

If You Want to Find Alternative Treatment

Many health professionals believe an integrative approach is the best way to treat eating disorders, so most treatment facilities offer some form of alternative treatment options. Something Fishy Web site on Eating Disorders offers a comprehensive directory of facilities that offer holistic or alternative treatment. Visit www.something-fishy.org/treatmentfinder/Category/Holistic--Alternative/

If You Have a Relapse

If you have a relapse and slip into old eating behaviors, it is important to have supports to reach out to. If you don't have friends or family who can give you the help you need, there are a number of hotlines you can call:

NEDA Helpline: 1-800-931-2237

Bulimia and Self-Help Hotline: 1-314-588-1683

For a comprehensive list of hotlines and referral services, visit www.something-fishy.org/other/hotlines.php

GLOSSARY

amenorrhea
The absence of menstruation for at least three months.

antidepressant
A drug used to treat or prevent clinical depression that works by altering the function of brain neurotransmitters.

concordance
When the same genetic trait appears in both twins in a pair.

dehydration
Abnormal and excessive loss of water from the body.

diuretic
A drug taken to increase urination.

enzyme
Any of various proteins that facilitate important chemical reactions in the body.

glaucoma
An eye disease with symptoms that include abnormally high intraocular fluid pressure, damaged optic disk, hardening of the eyeball, and partial to complete loss of vision.

hormone
A chemical produced by an endocrine gland that travels through the bloodstream and controls body processes, including mood and behavior.

insulin
A hormone secreted by the pancreas that regulates blood sugar and allows glucose to be converted into energy.

lanugo
The growth of fine downy hair on the body, a symptom of malnutrition.

laxative
A medication taken to relieve constipation.

malnutrition
A health condition that occurs when the body is starved of essential nutrients. It can result in organ failure and death.

muscle atrophy
The wasting of body muscle mass due to malnourishment.

obesity
The unhealthy, excessive accumulation and storage of body fat.

osteoporosis
A condition in which bones become weak and break easily.

pancreatitis
Inflammation of the pancreas.

ADDITIONAL RESOURCES

SELECTED BIBLIOGRAPHY

Abraham, Suzanne. *Eating Disorders: The Facts*. New York: Oxford, 2008. Print.

Best-Boss, Angie. *The Everything Parent's Guide to Eating Disorders*. Avon, MA: Adams Media, 2012. Print.

"Eating Disorders." *American Psychiatric Association*. American Psychiatric Association, 2012. Web. 20 Apr. 2013.

"Eating Disorders Statistics." *ANAD.org*. National Association of Anorexia Nervosa and Associated Disorders, 2013. Web. 18 May 2013.

"Feeding and Eating Disorders" 2013. *DSM-5*. PDF file. 20 Apr. 2013.

Judd, Sandra J., ed. *Eating Disorders Sourcebook*. Detroit: Omnigraphics, 2011. Print.

FURTHER READINGS

Bellenir, Elizabeth, ed. *Eating Disorders Information for Teens*. Detroit, MI: Omnigraphics, 2013. Print.

Marsico, Katie. *Eating Disorders*. New York: Marshall Cavendish, 2013. Print.

Orr, Tamra. *When the Mirror Lies: Anorexia, Bulimia, and Other Eating Disorders*. Danbury, CT: Franklin Watts, 2007. Print.

Parks, Peggy J. *Teenage Eating Disorders*. San Diego, CA: ReferencePoint, 2012. Print.

Peters, Celeste A. *Health Q & A*. New York: Weigl, 2013. Print.

WEB SITES

To learn more about living with eating disorders, visit ABDO Publishing Company online at **www.abdopublishing.com**. Web sites about living with eating disorders are featured on our Book Links page. These links are routinely monitored and updated to provide the most current information available.

SOURCE NOTES

CHAPTER 1. WARNING SIGNS AND SYMPTOMS

1. "Eating Disorder Statistics." *Mirasol Recovery Centers.* Mirasol, 2013. Web. 13 Apr. 2013.

2. "Eating Disorders Statistics." *National Association of Anorexia and Associated Disorders.* National Association of Anorexia and Associated Disorders, 2013. Web. 18 May 2013.

3. Leslie A. Sim, et al. "Identification and Treatment of Eating Disorders in the Primary Care Setting." *Mayo Clinic Proceedings.* US National Library of Medicine, 2010. Web. 28 Apr. 2013.

4. "Feeding and Eating Disorders." 2013. *DSM-5.* PDF file. 20 Apr. 2013.

5. "Eating Disorder Statistics." *Mirasol Recovery Centers.* Mirasol, 2013. Web. 13 Apr. 2013.

6. Kirsten Weir. "Big Kids." *American Psychological Association.* American Psychological Association, Dec. 2012. Web. 28 Apr. 2013.

7. "Eating Disorder Statistics." *Mirasol Recovery Centers.* Mirasol, 2013. Web. 13 Apr. 2013.

CHAPTER 2. CAUSES AND RISK FACTORS

1. "Eating Disorders Statistics." *National Association of Anorexia and Associated Disorders.* National Association of Anorexia and Associated Disorders, 2013. Web. 18 May 2013.

2. Kathleen N. Franco. "Eating Disorders." *Cleveland Clinic.* Cleveland Clinic Foundation, 2013. Web. 15 Apr. 2013.

3. "Eating Disorders Statistics." *National Association of Anorexia and Associated Disorders.* National Association of Anorexia and Associated Disorders, 2013. Web. 18 May 2013.

4. "Eating Disorder Statistics." *Mirasol Recovery Centers*. Mirasol, 2013. Web. 13 Apr. 2013.

5. Sharon Kirkey. "Anorexia Hitting Men Increasingly Hard: One in Three Cases in New Study Is Male." *Health*. National Post, 21 Jan. 2013. Web. 13 Apr. 2013.

6. "Eating Disorder Statistics." *Mirasol Recovery Centers*. Mirasol, 2013. Web. 13 Apr. 2013.

7. "Eating Disorders Statistics." *National Association of Anorexia and Associated Disorders*. National Association of Anorexia and Associated Disorders, 2013. Web. 18 May 2013.

8. "Eating Disorder Statistics." *Mirasol Recovery Centers*. Mirasol, 2013. Web. 13 Apr. 2013.

9. Ibid.

10. W. H. Kaye, et al. "Comorbidity of Anxiety Disorders with Anorexia and Bulimia Nervosa." *PubMed.gov*. US National Library of Medicine, Dec. 2004. Web. 11 May 2013.

11. Giulio Disanto, et al. "Season of Birth and Anorexia Nervosa." *The British Journal of Psychiatry*. The Royal College of Psychiatrists, 2013. Web. 9 May 2013.

CHAPTER 3. COMPLICATIONS

1. "30% of Women Would Trade at Least One Year of Their Life to Achieve Their Ideal Body Weight and Shape." *University of the West of England.* University of the West of England, 31 Mar. 2011. Web. 8 June 2013.

SOURCE NOTES CONTINUED

CHAPTER 4. TESTS AND DIAGNOSIS

1. "Eating Disorders Statistics." *National Association of Anorexia and Associated Disorders.* National Association of Anorexia and Associated Disorders, 2013. Web. 18 May 2013.

2. "Eating Disorders." *University of Maryland Medical Center.* University of Maryland Medical Center, 2011. Web. 1 June 2013.

3. R. Marsh, et al. "Deficient Activity in the Neural Systems that Mediate Self-Regulatory Control in Bulimia Nervosa." *PubMed*.gov. US National Library of Medicine, 2009. Web. 17 May 2013.

CHAPTER 5. TREATMENT

1. Brenda M. Malinauskas, et al. "Dieting Practices, Weight Perceptions, and Body Composition: A Comparison of Normal Weight, Overweight, and Obese College Females." *Nutrition Journal.* BioMed Central, 31 Mar. 2006. Web. 18 May 2013.

2. Daniel Le Grange and James Lock. "Family-Based Treatment of Adolescent Anorexia Nervosa: The Maudsley Approach" *Maudsley Parents*, n.d. Web. 18 May 2013.

3. Amy Novotney. "New Solutions." *American Psychological Association.* American Psychological Association, Apr. 2009. Web. 17 May 2013.

4. "Eating Disorder Statistics." *Mirasol Recovery Centers.* Mirasol, 2013. Web. 13 Apr. 2013.

5. "Facts About Eating Disorders: What the Research Shows." *Eating Disorders Coalition*, n.d. PDF file. 18 May 2013.

CHAPTER 6. HOME AND LIFESTYLE CHANGES

1. "Adventure-Based Therapy for Eating Disorders." *Mirasol Recovery Centers*. Mirasol, 2013. Web. 13 Apr. 2013.

2. Brandi-Ann Uyemura. "The Truth About Animal-Assisted Therapy." *Psych Central*. Pysch Central, 2011. Web. 1 June 2013.

CHAPTER 7. COPING AND SUPPORT

1. "Eating Disorders: A Guide to Coping Strategies." *UW Health.org*. University of Wisconsin Hospitals and Clinics, 14 Apr. 2010. Web. 18 May 2013.

CHAPTER 8. HELPING SOMEONE ELSE: REACHING OUT

1. "Facts About Eating Disorders: What the Research Shows." *Eating Disorders Coalition*, n.d. PDF file. 18 May 2013.

CHAPTER 9. PREVENTION

1. "Real Girls, Real Pressure: A National Report on the State of Self-Esteem." *The Dove Self-Esteem Fund*, n.d. PDF file. 19 May 2013.

2. Barbie Latza Nadeau. "Isabelle Caro: Anorexic Model Dies, Her Mother Commits Suicide. How Should the Fashion Industry Respond?" *Daily Beast*. Newsweek/Daily Beast, 7 Feb. 2011. Web. 18 May 2013.

3. Heather Shaw, et al. "Preventing Eating Disorders." *NIH.gov*. US National Library of Medicine, 18 Jan. 2009. Web. 19 May 2013.

4. Susan Paxton, et al. Letter to Michelle Obama. 7 Jan. 2009. *Eating Disorders Coalition*, n.d. PDF file. 18 May 2013.

INDEX

ABOUT THE AUTHOR

Racquel Foran is a freelance writer who lives in British Columbia, Canada. In addition to having written a number of juvenile reference books on topics as varied as developing nations' debt, North Korea, and organ transplants, Foran is the publisher and managing editor of a dance magazine that also targets juvenile readers. She is passionate about fostering a love of reading and learning in children.